STUDENT NAME _____

PHONE NUMBER _____

TEACHER NAME _____

PHONE NUMBER _____

Musician's
Practice
Planner

A WEEKLY LESSON PLANNER
FOR MUSIC STUDENTS

MoltoMusic
MOLTO MUSIC PUBLISHING COMPANY

Exclusively Distributed By

HAL•LEONARD®
CORPORATION
7777 W. BLUEMOUND RD. P.O. BOX 13819 MILWAUKEE, WI 53213

Music teachers often need a practical means of communicating their assignments and a simple way of helping their students develop better practice habits. The **Musician's Practice Planner** meets both needs.

The Musician's Practice Planner is easy to use and will increase the efficiency of your teaching. Simply fill out the **Weekly Lesson Plan** at each lesson. The broad categories let you customize the Weekly Lesson Plan to suit your personal teaching style and meet the needs of each of your students. There is even space to write out a short musical example. In the back of the Musician's Practice Planner, you will find additional staff paper.

The **Daily Practice Log** is filled out between lessons by the student. The log helps students focus during their practice sessions and gives teachers insight into the usually private world of the practice room.

By using the Musician's Practice Planner your students will learn more, practice more, and remember more. Both teacher and student can see exactly what was covered at the previous lesson and what the expectations are for the current lesson. The Musician's Practice Planner motivates students so they will improve faster than ever before.

Here are some of the many ways music teachers use the Musician's Practice Planner:

SCALES AND WARMUPS	SPECIFIC GOALS
Use this space for items that begin a practice session: • Scales, modes, and arpeggios • Dexterity and long tone exercises • Drum rudiments	*You can offer general technical guidance here:* • Posture • Hand and finger positions • Breathing and embouchure • Intonation and vibrato
ETUDES AND EXERCISES	SPECIFIC GOALS
Your students can look here for pages and exercise numbers: • Sightreading • Etudes and Technical Studies • Method book assignments	*Guide your students through the challenges of each technical exercise:* • Mastering difficult techniques • Working with a metronome • Counting while playing
REPERTOIRE	SPECIFIC GOALS
Assign performance pieces: • Solo and ensemble pieces • Jazz standards • Rock and popular songs	*Help students with performance skills:* • Phrasing and dynamics • Tempos and transitions • What to memorize
OTHER	SPECIFIC GOALS
List any other assignments for the week: • Theory exercises • Listening • Rhythm and metronome drills • Transcriptions	*Remind students that there's more than just performing:* • Improving musicianship skills away from your instrument • Memorizing keys and time signatures

SPECIAL NOTES FOR THE WEEK

You can include general reminders in this special notes section:

• Words of encouragement

• Notes to parents

• Accessories, books, and recordings to purchase

The **Musician's Practice Planner** is designed to help you get more out of practicing. Using it can help you become a better musician faster than ever before. Here's how the Practice Planner works:

Your teacher fills out the left page (the **Weekly Lesson Plan**) at your lesson. The Weekly Lesson Plan is a list of exactly what you need to practice. Since you're on your own while practicing, it's nice to have a reminder of what to work on.

Between lessons you fill out the right page (the **Daily Practice Log**). Each day, look over your teacher's notes in the Weekly Lesson Plan and decide what you want to practice. Write down these items in the Practice Priorities section. This way, you'll know just what you want to accomplish while you practice.

In the Practice Planner you can keep track of how much time you spend practicing and how fast you can play each piece. Writing down your practice times and seeing them at the end of the week will give you a sense of satisfaction. And, you'll be surprised how quickly you improve.

Here are a few suggestions for using the Practice Planner:

Make a list of what you'll be practicing today. Your list might look something like this:

Keep track of how fast you can easily play each piece of music.

List how much time you spent on each item.

Write down how much you practiced today.

PRACTICE PRIORITIES	METRONOME MARKING	TIME SPENT	TOTAL PRACTICE TIME
C Major Scale	♩ = 80	5 min.	
Method Book pg. 10, #7, first 16 bars	♩ = 104	15 min.	day 1
Solo piece: 2nd movement	♩ = 60	30 min.	50 min.

PRACTICE PRIORITIES	METRONOME MARKING	TIME SPENT	TOTAL PRACTICE TIME
C Major Scale and arpeggio	♩ = 84	5 min.	
Method Book pg. 10, #7, first 32 bars	♩ = 104	30 min.	day 2
Solo piece: 2nd mvmt	♩ = 66	5 min.	45 min.
3rd mvmt	♩ = 120	5 min.	

The next day, you'll want to review what you did yesterday as well as work on something new.

Try to reach your tempo goals each day.

This column shows if you are focusing on one of your practice priorities at the expense of the others.

Try to spend time practicing every day. It's better to practice a small amount each day than a huge amount one day per week.

WEEKLY LESSON PLAN

TODAY'S DATE: _____

SCALES AND WARMUPS	SPECIFIC GOALS

ETUDES AND EXERCISES	SPECIFIC GOALS

REPERTOIRE	SPECIFIC GOALS

OTHER	SPECIFIC GOALS

SPECIAL NOTES FOR THE WEEK

NEXT LESSON

Date:

Time:

PLEASE BRING TO YOUR NEXT LESSON

PRACTICE PRIORITIES	METRONOME MARKING	TIME SPENT	TOTAL PRACTICE TIME
			day 1

PRACTICE PRIORITIES	METRONOME MARKING	TIME SPENT	TOTAL PRACTICE TIME
			day 2

PRACTICE PRIORITIES	METRONOME MARKING	TIME SPENT	TOTAL PRACTICE TIME
			day 3

PRACTICE PRIORITIES	METRONOME MARKING	TIME SPENT	TOTAL PRACTICE TIME
			day 4

PRACTICE PRIORITIES	METRONOME MARKING	TIME SPENT	TOTAL PRACTICE TIME
			day 5

PRACTICE PRIORITIES	METRONOME MARKING	TIME SPENT	TOTAL PRACTICE TIME
			day 6

PRACTICE PRIORITIES	METRONOME MARKING	TIME SPENT	TOTAL PRACTICE TIME
			day 7

WEEKLY LESSON PLAN

TODAY'S DATE: _____

SCALES AND WARMUPS	SPECIFIC GOALS

ETUDES AND EXERCISES	SPECIFIC GOALS

REPERTOIRE	SPECIFIC GOALS

OTHER	SPECIFIC GOALS

SPECIAL NOTES FOR THE WEEK

NEXT LESSON

Date:

Time:

PLEASE BRING TO YOUR NEXT LESSON

PRACTICE PRIORITIES	METRONOME MARKING	TIME SPENT	TOTAL PRACTICE TIME
			day 1
PRACTICE PRIORITIES	METRONOME MARKING	TIME SPENT	TOTAL PRACTICE TIME
			day 2
PRACTICE PRIORITIES	METRONOME MARKING	TIME SPENT	TOTAL PRACTICE TIME
			day 3
PRACTICE PRIORITIES	METRONOME MARKING	TIME SPENT	TOTAL PRACTICE TIME
			day 4
PRACTICE PRIORITIES	METRONOME MARKING	TIME SPENT	TOTAL PRACTICE TIME
			day 5
PRACTICE PRIORITIES	METRONOME MARKING	TIME SPENT	TOTAL PRACTICE TIME
			day 6
PRACTICE PRIORITIES	METRONOME MARKING	TIME SPENT	TOTAL PRACTICE TIME
			day 7

WEEKLY LESSON PLAN

TODAY'S DATE:

SCALES AND WARMUPS	SPECIFIC GOALS
ETUDES AND EXERCISES	SPECIFIC GOALS
REPERTOIRE	SPECIFIC GOALS
OTHER	SPECIFIC GOALS

SPECIAL NOTES FOR THE WEEK

NEXT LESSON

Date:

Time:

PLEASE BRING TO YOUR NEXT LESSON

PRACTICE PRIORITIES	METRONOME MARKING	TIME SPENT	TOTAL PRACTICE TIME
			day 1
PRACTICE PRIORITIES	METRONOME MARKING	TIME SPENT	TOTAL PRACTICE TIME
			day 2
PRACTICE PRIORITIES	METRONOME MARKING	TIME SPENT	TOTAL PRACTICE TIME
			day 3
PRACTICE PRIORITIES	METRONOME MARKING	TIME SPENT	TOTAL PRACTICE TIME
			day 4
PRACTICE PRIORITIES	METRONOME MARKING	TIME SPENT	TOTAL PRACTICE TIME
			day 5
PRACTICE PRIORITIES	METRONOME MARKING	TIME SPENT	TOTAL PRACTICE TIME
			day 6
PRACTICE PRIORITIES	METRONOME MARKING	TIME SPENT	TOTAL PRACTICE TIME
			day 7

WEEKLY LESSON PLAN

TODAY'S DATE: _____

SCALES AND WARMUPS	SPECIFIC GOALS
ETUDES AND EXERCISES	SPECIFIC GOALS
REPERTOIRE	SPECIFIC GOALS
OTHER	SPECIFIC GOALS

SPECIAL NOTES FOR THE WEEK

NEXT LESSON

Date:

Time:

PLEASE BRING TO YOUR NEXT LESSON

PRACTICE PRIORITIES	METRONOME MARKING	TIME SPENT	TOTAL PRACTICE TIME
			day 1
PRACTICE PRIORITIES	METRONOME MARKING	TIME SPENT	TOTAL PRACTICE TIME
			day 2
PRACTICE PRIORITIES	METRONOME MARKING	TIME SPENT	TOTAL PRACTICE TIME
			day 3
PRACTICE PRIORITIES	METRONOME MARKING	TIME SPENT	TOTAL PRACTICE TIME
			day 4
PRACTICE PRIORITIES	METRONOME MARKING	TIME SPENT	TOTAL PRACTICE TIME
			day 5
PRACTICE PRIORITIES	METRONOME MARKING	TIME SPENT	TOTAL PRACTICE TIME
			day 6
PRACTICE PRIORITIES	METRONOME MARKING	TIME SPENT	TOTAL PRACTICE TIME
			day 7

WEEKLY LESSON PLAN

TODAY'S DATE: _____

SCALES AND WARMUPS	SPECIFIC GOALS

ETUDES AND EXERCISES	SPECIFIC GOALS

REPERTOIRE	SPECIFIC GOALS

OTHER	SPECIFIC GOALS

SPECIAL NOTES FOR THE WEEK

NEXT LESSON

Date:

Time:

PLEASE BRING TO YOUR NEXT LESSON

PRACTICE PRIORITIES	METRONOME MARKING	TIME SPENT	TOTAL PRACTICE TIME
			day 1
PRACTICE PRIORITIES	METRONOME MARKING	TIME SPENT	TOTAL PRACTICE TIME
			day 2
PRACTICE PRIORITIES	METRONOME MARKING	TIME SPENT	TOTAL PRACTICE TIME
			day 3
PRACTICE PRIORITIES	METRONOME MARKING	TIME SPENT	TOTAL PRACTICE TIME
			day 4
PRACTICE PRIORITIES	METRONOME MARKING	TIME SPENT	TOTAL PRACTICE TIME
			day 5
PRACTICE PRIORITIES	METRONOME MARKING	TIME SPENT	TOTAL PRACTICE TIME
			day 6
PRACTICE PRIORITIES	METRONOME MARKING	TIME SPENT	TOTAL PRACTICE TIME
			day 7

WEEKLY LESSON PLAN

TODAY'S DATE:

SCALES AND WARMUPS	SPECIFIC GOALS

ETUDES AND EXERCISES	SPECIFIC GOALS

REPERTOIRE	SPECIFIC GOALS

OTHER	SPECIFIC GOALS

SPECIAL NOTES FOR THE WEEK

NEXT LESSON

Date:

Time:

PLEASE BRING TO YOUR NEXT LESSON

PRACTICE PRIORITIES	METRONOME MARKING	TIME SPENT	TOTAL PRACTICE TIME
			day 1
PRACTICE PRIORITIES	METRONOME MARKING	TIME SPENT	TOTAL PRACTICE TIME
			day 2
PRACTICE PRIORITIES	METRONOME MARKING	TIME SPENT	TOTAL PRACTICE TIME
			day 3
PRACTICE PRIORITIES	METRONOME MARKING	TIME SPENT	TOTAL PRACTICE TIME
			day 4
PRACTICE PRIORITIES	METRONOME MARKING	TIME SPENT	TOTAL PRACTICE TIME
			day 5
PRACTICE PRIORITIES	METRONOME MARKING	TIME SPENT	TOTAL PRACTICE TIME
			day 6
PRACTICE PRIORITIES	METRONOME MARKING	TIME SPENT	TOTAL PRACTICE TIME
			day 7

WEEKLY LESSON PLAN

TODAY'S DATE:

| SCALES AND WARMUPS | SPECIFIC GOALS |

| ETUDES AND EXERCISES | SPECIFIC GOALS |

| REPERTOIRE | SPECIFIC GOALS |

| OTHER | SPECIFIC GOALS |

SPECIAL NOTES FOR THE WEEK

NEXT LESSON

Date:

Time:

PLEASE BRING TO YOUR NEXT LESSON

PRACTICE PRIORITIES	METRONOME MARKING	TIME SPENT	TOTAL PRACTICE TIME
			day 1
PRACTICE PRIORITIES	METRONOME MARKING	TIME SPENT	TOTAL PRACTICE TIME
			day 2
PRACTICE PRIORITIES	METRONOME MARKING	TIME SPENT	TOTAL PRACTICE TIME
			day 3
PRACTICE PRIORITIES	METRONOME MARKING	TIME SPENT	TOTAL PRACTICE TIME
			day 4
PRACTICE PRIORITIES	METRONOME MARKING	TIME SPENT	TOTAL PRACTICE TIME
			day 5
PRACTICE PRIORITIES	METRONOME MARKING	TIME SPENT	TOTAL PRACTICE TIME
			day 6
PRACTICE PRIORITIES	METRONOME MARKING	TIME SPENT	TOTAL PRACTICE TIME
			day 7

WEEKLY LESSON PLAN

TODAY'S DATE:

SCALES AND WARMUPS	SPECIFIC GOALS
ETUDES AND EXERCISES	SPECIFIC GOALS
REPERTOIRE	SPECIFIC GOALS
OTHER	SPECIFIC GOALS

SPECIAL NOTES FOR THE WEEK

NEXT LESSON

Date:

Time:

PLEASE BRING TO YOUR NEXT LESSON

PRACTICE PRIORITIES	METRONOME MARKING	TIME SPENT	TOTAL PRACTICE TIME
			day 1
PRACTICE PRIORITIES	METRONOME MARKING	TIME SPENT	TOTAL PRACTICE TIME
			day 2
PRACTICE PRIORITIES	METRONOME MARKING	TIME SPENT	TOTAL PRACTICE TIME
			day 3
PRACTICE PRIORITIES	METRONOME MARKING	TIME SPENT	TOTAL PRACTICE TIME
			day 4
PRACTICE PRIORITIES	METRONOME MARKING	TIME SPENT	TOTAL PRACTICE TIME
			day 5
PRACTICE PRIORITIES	METRONOME MARKING	TIME SPENT	TOTAL PRACTICE TIME
			day 6
PRACTICE PRIORITIES	METRONOME MARKING	TIME SPENT	TOTAL PRACTICE TIME
			day 7

TODAY'S DATE:

SCALES AND WARMUPS	SPECIFIC GOALS

ETUDES AND EXERCISES	SPECIFIC GOALS

REPERTOIRE	SPECIFIC GOALS

OTHER	SPECIFIC GOALS

SPECIAL NOTES FOR THE WEEK

NEXT LESSON	PLEASE BRING TO YOUR NEXT LESSON
Date:	
Time:	

PRACTICE PRIORITIES	METRONOME MARKING	TIME SPENT	TOTAL PRACTICE TIME
			day 1
PRACTICE PRIORITIES	METRONOME MARKING	TIME SPENT	TOTAL PRACTICE TIME
			day 2
PRACTICE PRIORITIES	METRONOME MARKING	TIME SPENT	TOTAL PRACTICE TIME
			day 3
PRACTICE PRIORITIES	METRONOME MARKING	TIME SPENT	TOTAL PRACTICE TIME
			day 4
PRACTICE PRIORITIES	METRONOME MARKING	TIME SPENT	TOTAL PRACTICE TIME
			day 5
PRACTICE PRIORITIES	METRONOME MARKING	TIME SPENT	TOTAL PRACTICE TIME
			day 6
PRACTICE PRIORITIES	METRONOME MARKING	TIME SPENT	TOTAL PRACTICE TIME
			day 7

WEEKLY LESSON PLAN

TODAY'S DATE: _____

SCALES AND WARMUPS	SPECIFIC GOALS

ETUDES AND EXERCISES	SPECIFIC GOALS

REPERTOIRE	SPECIFIC GOALS

OTHER	SPECIFIC GOALS

SPECIAL NOTES FOR THE WEEK

NEXT LESSON

Date:

Time:

PLEASE BRING TO YOUR NEXT LESSON

PRACTICE PRIORITIES	METRONOME MARKING	TIME SPENT	TOTAL PRACTICE TIME
			day 1
PRACTICE PRIORITIES	METRONOME MARKING	TIME SPENT	TOTAL PRACTICE TIME
			day 2
PRACTICE PRIORITIES	METRONOME MARKING	TIME SPENT	TOTAL PRACTICE TIME
			day 3
PRACTICE PRIORITIES	METRONOME MARKING	TIME SPENT	TOTAL PRACTICE TIME
			day 4
PRACTICE PRIORITIES	METRONOME MARKING	TIME SPENT	TOTAL PRACTICE TIME
			day 5
PRACTICE PRIORITIES	METRONOME MARKING	TIME SPENT	TOTAL PRACTICE TIME
			day 6
PRACTICE PRIORITIES	METRONOME MARKING	TIME SPENT	TOTAL PRACTICE TIME
			day 7

WEEKLY LESSON PLAN

TODAY'S DATE:

SCALES AND WARMUPS	SPECIFIC GOALS

ETUDES AND EXERCISES	SPECIFIC GOALS

REPERTOIRE	SPECIFIC GOALS

OTHER	SPECIFIC GOALS

SPECIAL NOTES FOR THE WEEK

NEXT LESSON	PLEASE BRING TO YOUR NEXT LESSON
Date:	
Time:	

PRACTICE PRIORITIES	METRONOME MARKING	TIME SPENT	TOTAL PRACTICE TIME
			day 1
PRACTICE PRIORITIES	METRONOME MARKING	TIME SPENT	TOTAL PRACTICE TIME
			day 2
PRACTICE PRIORITIES	METRONOME MARKING	TIME SPENT	TOTAL PRACTICE TIME
			day 3
PRACTICE PRIORITIES	METRONOME MARKING	TIME SPENT	TOTAL PRACTICE TIME
			day 4
PRACTICE PRIORITIES	METRONOME MARKING	TIME SPENT	TOTAL PRACTICE TIME
			day 5
PRACTICE PRIORITIES	METRONOME MARKING	TIME SPENT	TOTAL PRACTICE TIME
			day 6
PRACTICE PRIORITIES	METRONOME MARKING	TIME SPENT	TOTAL PRACTICE TIME
			day 7

WEEKLY LESSON PLAN

TODAY'S DATE:

SCALES AND WARMUPS	SPECIFIC GOALS
ETUDES AND EXERCISES	SPECIFIC GOALS
REPERTOIRE	SPECIFIC GOALS
OTHER	SPECIFIC GOALS

SPECIAL NOTES FOR THE WEEK

NEXT LESSON

Date:

Time:

PLEASE BRING TO YOUR NEXT LESSON

PRACTICE PRIORITIES	METRONOME MARKING	TIME SPENT	TOTAL PRACTICE TIME
			day 1

PRACTICE PRIORITIES	METRONOME MARKING	TIME SPENT	TOTAL PRACTICE TIME
			day 2

PRACTICE PRIORITIES	METRONOME MARKING	TIME SPENT	TOTAL PRACTICE TIME
			day 3

PRACTICE PRIORITIES	METRONOME MARKING	TIME SPENT	TOTAL PRACTICE TIME
			day 4

PRACTICE PRIORITIES	METRONOME MARKING	TIME SPENT	TOTAL PRACTICE TIME
			day 5

PRACTICE PRIORITIES	METRONOME MARKING	TIME SPENT	TOTAL PRACTICE TIME
			day 6

PRACTICE PRIORITIES	METRONOME MARKING	TIME SPENT	TOTAL PRACTICE TIME
			day 7

WEEKLY LESSON PLAN

TODAY'S DATE:

SCALES AND WARMUPS	SPECIFIC GOALS

ETUDES AND EXERCISES	SPECIFIC GOALS

REPERTOIRE	SPECIFIC GOALS

OTHER	SPECIFIC GOALS

SPECIAL NOTES FOR THE WEEK

NEXT LESSON

Date:

Time:

PLEASE BRING TO YOUR NEXT LESSON

PRACTICE PRIORITIES	METRONOME MARKING	TIME SPENT	TOTAL PRACTICE TIME
			day 1

PRACTICE PRIORITIES	METRONOME MARKING	TIME SPENT	TOTAL PRACTICE TIME
			day 2

PRACTICE PRIORITIES	METRONOME MARKING	TIME SPENT	TOTAL PRACTICE TIME
			day 3

PRACTICE PRIORITIES	METRONOME MARKING	TIME SPENT	TOTAL PRACTICE TIME
			day 4

PRACTICE PRIORITIES	METRONOME MARKING	TIME SPENT	TOTAL PRACTICE TIME
			day 5

PRACTICE PRIORITIES	METRONOME MARKING	TIME SPENT	TOTAL PRACTICE TIME
			day 6

PRACTICE PRIORITIES	METRONOME MARKING	TIME SPENT	TOTAL PRACTICE TIME
			day 7

WEEKLY LESSON PLAN

TODAY'S DATE:

SCALES AND WARMUPS	SPECIFIC GOALS

ETUDES AND EXERCISES	SPECIFIC GOALS

REPERTOIRE	SPECIFIC GOALS

OTHER	SPECIFIC GOALS

SPECIAL NOTES FOR THE WEEK

NEXT LESSON

Date:

Time:

PLEASE BRING TO YOUR NEXT LESSON

PRACTICE PRIORITIES	METRONOME MARKING	TIME SPENT	TOTAL PRACTICE TIME
			day 1

PRACTICE PRIORITIES	METRONOME MARKING	TIME SPENT	TOTAL PRACTICE TIME
			day 2

PRACTICE PRIORITIES	METRONOME MARKING	TIME SPENT	TOTAL PRACTICE TIME
			day 3

PRACTICE PRIORITIES	METRONOME MARKING	TIME SPENT	TOTAL PRACTICE TIME
			day 4

PRACTICE PRIORITIES	METRONOME MARKING	TIME SPENT	TOTAL PRACTICE TIME
			day 5

PRACTICE PRIORITIES	METRONOME MARKING	TIME SPENT	TOTAL PRACTICE TIME
			day 6

PRACTICE PRIORITIES	METRONOME MARKING	TIME SPENT	TOTAL PRACTICE TIME
			day 7

WEEKLY LESSON PLAN

TODAY'S DATE:

SCALES AND WARMUPS	SPECIFIC GOALS
ETUDES AND EXERCISES	SPECIFIC GOALS
REPERTOIRE	SPECIFIC GOALS
OTHER	SPECIFIC GOALS

SPECIAL NOTES FOR THE WEEK

NEXT LESSON	PLEASE BRING TO YOUR NEXT LESSON
Date: Time:	

PRACTICE PRIORITIES	METRONOME MARKING	TIME SPENT	TOTAL PRACTICE TIME
			day 1
PRACTICE PRIORITIES	METRONOME MARKING	TIME SPENT	TOTAL PRACTICE TIME
			day 2
PRACTICE PRIORITIES	METRONOME MARKING	TIME SPENT	TOTAL PRACTICE TIME
			day 3
PRACTICE PRIORITIES	METRONOME MARKING	TIME SPENT	TOTAL PRACTICE TIME
			day 4
PRACTICE PRIORITIES	METRONOME MARKING	TIME SPENT	TOTAL PRACTICE TIME
			day 5
PRACTICE PRIORITIES	METRONOME MARKING	TIME SPENT	TOTAL PRACTICE TIME
			day 6
PRACTICE PRIORITIES	METRONOME MARKING	TIME SPENT	TOTAL PRACTICE TIME
			day 7

WEEKLY LESSON PLAN

TODAY'S DATE:

SCALES AND WARMUPS	SPECIFIC GOALS

ETUDES AND EXERCISES	SPECIFIC GOALS

REPERTOIRE	SPECIFIC GOALS

OTHER	SPECIFIC GOALS

SPECIAL NOTES FOR THE WEEK

NEXT LESSON

Date:

Time:

PLEASE BRING TO YOUR NEXT LESSON

PRACTICE PRIORITIES	METRONOME MARKING	TIME SPENT	TOTAL PRACTICE TIME

day 1

PRACTICE PRIORITIES	METRONOME MARKING	TIME SPENT	TOTAL PRACTICE TIME

day 2

PRACTICE PRIORITIES	METRONOME MARKING	TIME SPENT	TOTAL PRACTICE TIME

day 3

PRACTICE PRIORITIES	METRONOME MARKING	TIME SPENT	TOTAL PRACTICE TIME

day 4

PRACTICE PRIORITIES	METRONOME MARKING	TIME SPENT	TOTAL PRACTICE TIME

day 5

PRACTICE PRIORITIES	METRONOME MARKING	TIME SPENT	TOTAL PRACTICE TIME

day 6

PRACTICE PRIORITIES	METRONOME MARKING	TIME SPENT	TOTAL PRACTICE TIME

day 7

WEEKLY LESSON PLAN

TODAY'S DATE: _____

SCALES AND WARMUPS	SPECIFIC GOALS

ETUDES AND EXERCISES	SPECIFIC GOALS

REPERTOIRE	SPECIFIC GOALS

OTHER	SPECIFIC GOALS

SPECIAL NOTES FOR THE WEEK

NEXT LESSON

Date:

Time:

PLEASE BRING TO YOUR NEXT LESSON

PRACTICE PRIORITIES	METRONOME MARKING	TIME SPENT	TOTAL PRACTICE TIME
			day 1
PRACTICE PRIORITIES	METRONOME MARKING	TIME SPENT	TOTAL PRACTICE TIME
			day 2
PRACTICE PRIORITIES	METRONOME MARKING	TIME SPENT	TOTAL PRACTICE TIME
			day 3
PRACTICE PRIORITIES	METRONOME MARKING	TIME SPENT	TOTAL PRACTICE TIME
			day 4
PRACTICE PRIORITIES	METRONOME MARKING	TIME SPENT	TOTAL PRACTICE TIME
			day 5
PRACTICE PRIORITIES	METRONOME MARKING	TIME SPENT	TOTAL PRACTICE TIME
			day 6
PRACTICE PRIORITIES	METRONOME MARKING	TIME SPENT	TOTAL PRACTICE TIME
			day 7

WEEKLY LESSON PLAN

TODAY'S DATE:

| SCALES AND WARMUPS | SPECIFIC GOALS |

| ETUDES AND EXERCISES | SPECIFIC GOALS |

| REPERTOIRE | SPECIFIC GOALS |

| OTHER | SPECIFIC GOALS |

SPECIAL NOTES FOR THE WEEK

NEXT LESSON

Date:

Time:

PLEASE BRING TO YOUR NEXT LESSON

PRACTICE PRIORITIES	METRONOME MARKING	TIME SPENT	TOTAL PRACTICE TIME
			day 1

PRACTICE PRIORITIES	METRONOME MARKING	TIME SPENT	TOTAL PRACTICE TIME
			day 2

PRACTICE PRIORITIES	METRONOME MARKING	TIME SPENT	TOTAL PRACTICE TIME
			day 3

PRACTICE PRIORITIES	METRONOME MARKING	TIME SPENT	TOTAL PRACTICE TIME
			day 4

PRACTICE PRIORITIES	METRONOME MARKING	TIME SPENT	TOTAL PRACTICE TIME
			day 5

PRACTICE PRIORITIES	METRONOME MARKING	TIME SPENT	TOTAL PRACTICE TIME
			day 6

PRACTICE PRIORITIES	METRONOME MARKING	TIME SPENT	TOTAL PRACTICE TIME
			day 7

WEEKLY LESSON PLAN

TODAY'S DATE:

SCALES AND WARMUPS	SPECIFIC GOALS
ETUDES AND EXERCISES	SPECIFIC GOALS
REPERTOIRE	SPECIFIC GOALS
OTHER	SPECIFIC GOALS

SPECIAL NOTES FOR THE WEEK

NEXT LESSON

Date:

Time:

PLEASE BRING TO YOUR NEXT LESSON

PRACTICE PRIORITIES	METRONOME MARKING	TIME SPENT	TOTAL PRACTICE TIME
			day 1

PRACTICE PRIORITIES	METRONOME MARKING	TIME SPENT	TOTAL PRACTICE TIME
			day 2

PRACTICE PRIORITIES	METRONOME MARKING	TIME SPENT	TOTAL PRACTICE TIME
			day 3

PRACTICE PRIORITIES	METRONOME MARKING	TIME SPENT	TOTAL PRACTICE TIME
			day 4

PRACTICE PRIORITIES	METRONOME MARKING	TIME SPENT	TOTAL PRACTICE TIME
			day 5

PRACTICE PRIORITIES	METRONOME MARKING	TIME SPENT	TOTAL PRACTICE TIME
			day 6

PRACTICE PRIORITIES	METRONOME MARKING	TIME SPENT	TOTAL PRACTICE TIME
			day 7

WEEKLY LESSON PLAN

TODAY'S DATE:

SCALES AND WARMUPS	SPECIFIC GOALS

ETUDES AND EXERCISES	SPECIFIC GOALS

REPERTOIRE	SPECIFIC GOALS

OTHER	SPECIFIC GOALS

SPECIAL NOTES FOR THE WEEK

NEXT LESSON

Date:

Time:

PLEASE BRING TO YOUR NEXT LESSON

PRACTICE PRIORITIES	METRONOME MARKING	TIME SPENT	TOTAL PRACTICE TIME
			day 1
PRACTICE PRIORITIES	METRONOME MARKING	TIME SPENT	TOTAL PRACTICE TIME
			day 2
PRACTICE PRIORITIES	METRONOME MARKING	TIME SPENT	TOTAL PRACTICE TIME
			day 3
PRACTICE PRIORITIES	METRONOME MARKING	TIME SPENT	TOTAL PRACTICE TIME
			day 4
PRACTICE PRIORITIES	METRONOME MARKING	TIME SPENT	TOTAL PRACTICE TIME
			day 5
PRACTICE PRIORITIES	METRONOME MARKING	TIME SPENT	TOTAL PRACTICE TIME
			day 6
PRACTICE PRIORITIES	METRONOME MARKING	TIME SPENT	TOTAL PRACTICE TIME
			day 7

WEEKLY LESSON PLAN

TODAY'S DATE:

SCALES AND WARMUPS	SPECIFIC GOALS
ETUDES AND EXERCISES	SPECIFIC GOALS
REPERTOIRE	SPECIFIC GOALS
OTHER	SPECIFIC GOALS

SPECIAL NOTES FOR THE WEEK

NEXT LESSON

Date:

Time:

PLEASE BRING TO YOUR NEXT LESSON

PRACTICE PRIORITIES	METRONOME MARKING	TIME SPENT	TOTAL PRACTICE TIME
			day 1

PRACTICE PRIORITIES	METRONOME MARKING	TIME SPENT	TOTAL PRACTICE TIME
			day 2

PRACTICE PRIORITIES	METRONOME MARKING	TIME SPENT	TOTAL PRACTICE TIME
			day 3

PRACTICE PRIORITIES	METRONOME MARKING	TIME SPENT	TOTAL PRACTICE TIME
			day 4

PRACTICE PRIORITIES	METRONOME MARKING	TIME SPENT	TOTAL PRACTICE TIME
			day 5

PRACTICE PRIORITIES	METRONOME MARKING	TIME SPENT	TOTAL PRACTICE TIME
			day 6

PRACTICE PRIORITIES	METRONOME MARKING	TIME SPENT	TOTAL PRACTICE TIME
			day 7

WEEKLY LESSON PLAN

TODAY'S DATE:

SCALES AND WARMUPS	SPECIFIC GOALS

ETUDES AND EXERCISES	SPECIFIC GOALS

REPERTOIRE	SPECIFIC GOALS

OTHER	SPECIFIC GOALS

SPECIAL NOTES FOR THE WEEK

NEXT LESSON

Date:

Time:

PLEASE BRING TO YOUR NEXT LESSON

PRACTICE PRIORITIES	METRONOME MARKING	TIME SPENT	TOTAL PRACTICE TIME
			day 1

PRACTICE PRIORITIES	METRONOME MARKING	TIME SPENT	TOTAL PRACTICE TIME
			day 2

PRACTICE PRIORITIES	METRONOME MARKING	TIME SPENT	TOTAL PRACTICE TIME
			day 3

PRACTICE PRIORITIES	METRONOME MARKING	TIME SPENT	TOTAL PRACTICE TIME
			day 4

PRACTICE PRIORITIES	METRONOME MARKING	TIME SPENT	TOTAL PRACTICE TIME
			day 5

PRACTICE PRIORITIES	METRONOME MARKING	TIME SPENT	TOTAL PRACTICE TIME
			day 6

PRACTICE PRIORITIES	METRONOME MARKING	TIME SPENT	TOTAL PRACTICE TIME
			day 7

WEEKLY LESSON PLAN

TODAY'S DATE:

SCALES AND WARMUPS	SPECIFIC GOALS
ETUDES AND EXERCISES	SPECIFIC GOALS
REPERTOIRE	SPECIFIC GOALS
OTHER	SPECIFIC GOALS

SPECIAL NOTES FOR THE WEEK

NEXT LESSON

Date:

Time:

PLEASE BRING TO YOUR NEXT LESSON

PRACTICE PRIORITIES	METRONOME MARKING	TIME SPENT	TOTAL PRACTICE TIME
			day 1
PRACTICE PRIORITIES	METRONOME MARKING	TIME SPENT	TOTAL PRACTICE TIME
			day 2
PRACTICE PRIORITIES	METRONOME MARKING	TIME SPENT	TOTAL PRACTICE TIME
			day 3
PRACTICE PRIORITIES	METRONOME MARKING	TIME SPENT	TOTAL PRACTICE TIME
			day 4
PRACTICE PRIORITIES	METRONOME MARKING	TIME SPENT	TOTAL PRACTICE TIME
			day 5
PRACTICE PRIORITIES	METRONOME MARKING	TIME SPENT	TOTAL PRACTICE TIME
			day 6
PRACTICE PRIORITIES	METRONOME MARKING	TIME SPENT	TOTAL PRACTICE TIME
			day 7

WEEKLY LESSON PLAN

TODAY'S DATE:

SCALES AND WARMUPS	SPECIFIC GOALS

ETUDES AND EXERCISES	SPECIFIC GOALS

REPERTOIRE	SPECIFIC GOALS

OTHER	SPECIFIC GOALS

SPECIAL NOTES FOR THE WEEK

NEXT LESSON

Date:

Time:

PLEASE BRING TO YOUR NEXT LESSON

PRACTICE PRIORITIES	METRONOME MARKING	TIME SPENT	TOTAL PRACTICE TIME
			day 1
PRACTICE PRIORITIES	METRONOME MARKING	TIME SPENT	TOTAL PRACTICE TIME
			day 2
PRACTICE PRIORITIES	METRONOME MARKING	TIME SPENT	TOTAL PRACTICE TIME
			day 3
PRACTICE PRIORITIES	METRONOME MARKING	TIME SPENT	TOTAL PRACTICE TIME
			day 4
PRACTICE PRIORITIES	METRONOME MARKING	TIME SPENT	TOTAL PRACTICE TIME
			day 5
PRACTICE PRIORITIES	METRONOME MARKING	TIME SPENT	TOTAL PRACTICE TIME
			day 6
PRACTICE PRIORITIES	METRONOME MARKING	TIME SPENT	TOTAL PRACTICE TIME
			day 7

WEEKLY LESSON PLAN

TODAY'S DATE:

SCALES AND WARMUPS	SPECIFIC GOALS

ETUDES AND EXERCISES	SPECIFIC GOALS

REPERTOIRE	SPECIFIC GOALS

OTHER	SPECIFIC GOALS

SPECIAL NOTES FOR THE WEEK

NEXT LESSON

Date:

Time:

PLEASE BRING TO YOUR NEXT LESSON

PRACTICE PRIORITIES	METRONOME MARKING	TIME SPENT	TOTAL PRACTICE TIME
			day 1
PRACTICE PRIORITIES	METRONOME MARKING	TIME SPENT	TOTAL PRACTICE TIME
			day 2
PRACTICE PRIORITIES	METRONOME MARKING	TIME SPENT	TOTAL PRACTICE TIME
			day 3
PRACTICE PRIORITIES	METRONOME MARKING	TIME SPENT	TOTAL PRACTICE TIME
			day 4
PRACTICE PRIORITIES	METRONOME MARKING	TIME SPENT	TOTAL PRACTICE TIME
			day 5
PRACTICE PRIORITIES	METRONOME MARKING	TIME SPENT	TOTAL PRACTICE TIME
			day 6
PRACTICE PRIORITIES	METRONOME MARKING	TIME SPENT	TOTAL PRACTICE TIME
			day 7

TODAY'S DATE:

SCALES AND WARMUPS	SPECIFIC GOALS
ETUDES AND EXERCISES	SPECIFIC GOALS
REPERTOIRE	SPECIFIC GOALS
OTHER	SPECIFIC GOALS

SPECIAL NOTES FOR THE WEEK

NEXT LESSON

Date:

Time:

PLEASE BRING TO YOUR NEXT LESSON

PRACTICE PRIORITIES	METRONOME MARKING	TIME SPENT	TOTAL PRACTICE TIME
			day 1

PRACTICE PRIORITIES	METRONOME MARKING	TIME SPENT	TOTAL PRACTICE TIME
			day 2

PRACTICE PRIORITIES	METRONOME MARKING	TIME SPENT	TOTAL PRACTICE TIME
			day 3

PRACTICE PRIORITIES	METRONOME MARKING	TIME SPENT	TOTAL PRACTICE TIME
			day 4

PRACTICE PRIORITIES	METRONOME MARKING	TIME SPENT	TOTAL PRACTICE TIME
			day 5

PRACTICE PRIORITIES	METRONOME MARKING	TIME SPENT	TOTAL PRACTICE TIME
			day 6

PRACTICE PRIORITIES	METRONOME MARKING	TIME SPENT	TOTAL PRACTICE TIME
			day 7

WEEKLY LESSON PLAN

TODAY'S DATE:

SCALES AND WARMUPS

SPECIFIC GOALS

ETUDES AND EXERCISES

SPECIFIC GOALS

REPERTOIRE

SPECIFIC GOALS

OTHER

SPECIFIC GOALS

SPECIAL NOTES FOR THE WEEK

NEXT LESSON

Date:

Time:

PLEASE BRING TO YOUR NEXT LESSON

PRACTICE PRIORITIES	METRONOME MARKING	TIME SPENT	TOTAL PRACTICE TIME
			day 1

PRACTICE PRIORITIES	METRONOME MARKING	TIME SPENT	TOTAL PRACTICE TIME
			day 2

PRACTICE PRIORITIES	METRONOME MARKING	TIME SPENT	TOTAL PRACTICE TIME
			day 3

PRACTICE PRIORITIES	METRONOME MARKING	TIME SPENT	TOTAL PRACTICE TIME
			day 4

PRACTICE PRIORITIES	METRONOME MARKING	TIME SPENT	TOTAL PRACTICE TIME
			day 5

PRACTICE PRIORITIES	METRONOME MARKING	TIME SPENT	TOTAL PRACTICE TIME
			day 6

PRACTICE PRIORITIES	METRONOME MARKING	TIME SPENT	TOTAL PRACTICE TIME
			day 7

WEEKLY LESSON PLAN

TODAY'S DATE:

SCALES AND WARMUPS	SPECIFIC GOALS
ETUDES AND EXERCISES	SPECIFIC GOALS
REPERTOIRE	SPECIFIC GOALS
OTHER	SPECIFIC GOALS

SPECIAL NOTES FOR THE WEEK

NEXT LESSON

Date:

Time:

PLEASE BRING TO YOUR NEXT LESSON

PRACTICE PRIORITIES	METRONOME MARKING	TIME SPENT	TOTAL PRACTICE TIME
			day 1
PRACTICE PRIORITIES	METRONOME MARKING	TIME SPENT	TOTAL PRACTICE TIME
			day 2
PRACTICE PRIORITIES	METRONOME MARKING	TIME SPENT	TOTAL PRACTICE TIME
			day 3
PRACTICE PRIORITIES	METRONOME MARKING	TIME SPENT	TOTAL PRACTICE TIME
			day 4
PRACTICE PRIORITIES	METRONOME MARKING	TIME SPENT	TOTAL PRACTICE TIME
			day 5
PRACTICE PRIORITIES	METRONOME MARKING	TIME SPENT	TOTAL PRACTICE TIME
			day 6
PRACTICE PRIORITIES	METRONOME MARKING	TIME SPENT	TOTAL PRACTICE TIME
			day 7

WEEKLY LESSON PLAN

TODAY'S DATE: _____

SCALES AND WARMUPS	SPECIFIC GOALS

ETUDES AND EXERCISES	SPECIFIC GOALS

REPERTOIRE	SPECIFIC GOALS

OTHER	SPECIFIC GOALS

SPECIAL NOTES FOR THE WEEK

NEXT LESSON

Date:

Time:

PLEASE BRING TO YOUR NEXT LESSON

PRACTICE PRIORITIES	METRONOME MARKING	TIME SPENT	TOTAL PRACTICE TIME
			day 1
PRACTICE PRIORITIES	METRONOME MARKING	TIME SPENT	TOTAL PRACTICE TIME
			day 2
PRACTICE PRIORITIES	METRONOME MARKING	TIME SPENT	TOTAL PRACTICE TIME
			day 3
PRACTICE PRIORITIES	METRONOME MARKING	TIME SPENT	TOTAL PRACTICE TIME
			day 4
PRACTICE PRIORITIES	METRONOME MARKING	TIME SPENT	TOTAL PRACTICE TIME
			day 5
PRACTICE PRIORITIES	METRONOME MARKING	TIME SPENT	TOTAL PRACTICE TIME
			day 6
PRACTICE PRIORITIES	METRONOME MARKING	TIME SPENT	TOTAL PRACTICE TIME
			day 7

WEEKLY LESSON PLAN

TODAY'S DATE:

SCALES AND WARMUPS	SPECIFIC GOALS

ETUDES AND EXERCISES	SPECIFIC GOALS

REPERTOIRE	SPECIFIC GOALS

OTHER	SPECIFIC GOALS

SPECIAL NOTES FOR THE WEEK

NEXT LESSON

Date:

Time:

PLEASE BRING TO YOUR NEXT LESSON

PRACTICE PRIORITIES	METRONOME MARKING	TIME SPENT	TOTAL PRACTICE TIME
			day 1
PRACTICE PRIORITIES	METRONOME MARKING	TIME SPENT	TOTAL PRACTICE TIME
			day 2
PRACTICE PRIORITIES	METRONOME MARKING	TIME SPENT	TOTAL PRACTICE TIME
			day 3
PRACTICE PRIORITIES	METRONOME MARKING	TIME SPENT	TOTAL PRACTICE TIME
			day 4
PRACTICE PRIORITIES	METRONOME MARKING	TIME SPENT	TOTAL PRACTICE TIME
			day 5
PRACTICE PRIORITIES	METRONOME MARKING	TIME SPENT	TOTAL PRACTICE TIME
			day 6
PRACTICE PRIORITIES	METRONOME MARKING	TIME SPENT	TOTAL PRACTICE TIME
			day 7

WEEKLY LESSON PLAN

TODAY'S DATE:

SCALES AND WARMUPS	SPECIFIC GOALS
ETUDES AND EXERCISES	SPECIFIC GOALS
REPERTOIRE	SPECIFIC GOALS
OTHER	SPECIFIC GOALS

SPECIAL NOTES FOR THE WEEK

NEXT LESSON

Date:

Time:

PLEASE BRING TO YOUR NEXT LESSON

PRACTICE PRIORITIES	METRONOME MARKING	TIME SPENT	TOTAL PRACTICE TIME
			day 1
PRACTICE PRIORITIES	METRONOME MARKING	TIME SPENT	TOTAL PRACTICE TIME
			day 2
PRACTICE PRIORITIES	METRONOME MARKING	TIME SPENT	TOTAL PRACTICE TIME
			day 3
PRACTICE PRIORITIES	METRONOME MARKING	TIME SPENT	TOTAL PRACTICE TIME
			day 4
PRACTICE PRIORITIES	METRONOME MARKING	TIME SPENT	TOTAL PRACTICE TIME
			day 5
PRACTICE PRIORITIES	METRONOME MARKING	TIME SPENT	TOTAL PRACTICE TIME
			day 6
PRACTICE PRIORITIES	METRONOME MARKING	TIME SPENT	TOTAL PRACTICE TIME
			day 7

TODAY'S DATE:

SCALES AND WARMUPS	SPECIFIC GOALS

ETUDES AND EXERCISES	SPECIFIC GOALS

REPERTOIRE	SPECIFIC GOALS

OTHER	SPECIFIC GOALS

SPECIAL NOTES FOR THE WEEK

NEXT LESSON

Date:

Time:

PLEASE BRING TO YOUR NEXT LESSON

PRACTICE PRIORITIES	METRONOME MARKING	TIME SPENT	TOTAL PRACTICE TIME
			day 1
PRACTICE PRIORITIES	METRONOME MARKING	TIME SPENT	TOTAL PRACTICE TIME
			day 2
PRACTICE PRIORITIES	METRONOME MARKING	TIME SPENT	TOTAL PRACTICE TIME
			day 3
PRACTICE PRIORITIES	METRONOME MARKING	TIME SPENT	TOTAL PRACTICE TIME
			day 4
PRACTICE PRIORITIES	METRONOME MARKING	TIME SPENT	TOTAL PRACTICE TIME
			day 5
PRACTICE PRIORITIES	METRONOME MARKING	TIME SPENT	TOTAL PRACTICE TIME
			day 6
PRACTICE PRIORITIES	METRONOME MARKING	TIME SPENT	TOTAL PRACTICE TIME
			day 7

WEEKLY LESSON PLAN

TODAY'S DATE: _____

SCALES AND WARMUPS	SPECIFIC GOALS

ETUDES AND EXERCISES	SPECIFIC GOALS

REPERTOIRE	SPECIFIC GOALS

OTHER	SPECIFIC GOALS

SPECIAL NOTES FOR THE WEEK

NEXT LESSON

Date:

Time:

PLEASE BRING TO YOUR NEXT LESSON

PRACTICE PRIORITIES	METRONOME MARKING	TIME SPENT	TOTAL PRACTICE TIME
			day 1
PRACTICE PRIORITIES	METRONOME MARKING	TIME SPENT	TOTAL PRACTICE TIME
			day 2
PRACTICE PRIORITIES	METRONOME MARKING	TIME SPENT	TOTAL PRACTICE TIME
			day 3
PRACTICE PRIORITIES	METRONOME MARKING	TIME SPENT	TOTAL PRACTICE TIME
			day 4
PRACTICE PRIORITIES	METRONOME MARKING	TIME SPENT	TOTAL PRACTICE TIME
			day 5
PRACTICE PRIORITIES	METRONOME MARKING	TIME SPENT	TOTAL PRACTICE TIME
			day 6
PRACTICE PRIORITIES	METRONOME MARKING	TIME SPENT	TOTAL PRACTICE TIME
			day 7

WEEKLY LESSON PLAN

TODAY'S DATE:

SCALES AND WARMUPS	SPECIFIC GOALS
ETUDES AND EXERCISES	SPECIFIC GOALS
REPERTOIRE	SPECIFIC GOALS
OTHER	SPECIFIC GOALS

SPECIAL NOTES FOR THE WEEK

NEXT LESSON

Date:

Time:

PLEASE BRING TO YOUR NEXT LESSON

PRACTICE PRIORITIES	METRONOME MARKING	TIME SPENT	TOTAL PRACTICE TIME
			day 1

PRACTICE PRIORITIES	METRONOME MARKING	TIME SPENT	TOTAL PRACTICE TIME
			day 2

PRACTICE PRIORITIES	METRONOME MARKING	TIME SPENT	TOTAL PRACTICE TIME
			day 3

PRACTICE PRIORITIES	METRONOME MARKING	TIME SPENT	TOTAL PRACTICE TIME
			day 4

PRACTICE PRIORITIES	METRONOME MARKING	TIME SPENT	TOTAL PRACTICE TIME
			day 5

PRACTICE PRIORITIES	METRONOME MARKING	TIME SPENT	TOTAL PRACTICE TIME
			day 6

PRACTICE PRIORITIES	METRONOME MARKING	TIME SPENT	TOTAL PRACTICE TIME
			day 7

WEEKLY LESSON PLAN

TODAY'S DATE:

SCALES AND WARMUPS	SPECIFIC GOALS
ETUDES AND EXERCISES	**SPECIFIC GOALS**
REPERTOIRE	**SPECIFIC GOALS**
OTHER	**SPECIFIC GOALS**

SPECIAL NOTES FOR THE WEEK

NEXT LESSON	PLEASE BRING TO YOUR NEXT LESSON
Date:	
Time:	

PRACTICE PRIORITIES	METRONOME MARKING	TIME SPENT	TOTAL PRACTICE TIME
			day 1
PRACTICE PRIORITIES	METRONOME MARKING	TIME SPENT	TOTAL PRACTICE TIME
			day 2
PRACTICE PRIORITIES	METRONOME MARKING	TIME SPENT	TOTAL PRACTICE TIME
			day 3
PRACTICE PRIORITIES	METRONOME MARKING	TIME SPENT	TOTAL PRACTICE TIME
			day 4
PRACTICE PRIORITIES	METRONOME MARKING	TIME SPENT	TOTAL PRACTICE TIME
			day 5
PRACTICE PRIORITIES	METRONOME MARKING	TIME SPENT	TOTAL PRACTICE TIME
			day 6
PRACTICE PRIORITIES	METRONOME MARKING	TIME SPENT	TOTAL PRACTICE TIME
			day 7

TODAY'S DATE:

SCALES AND WARMUPS	SPECIFIC GOALS
ETUDES AND EXERCISES	SPECIFIC GOALS
REPERTOIRE	SPECIFIC GOALS
OTHER	SPECIFIC GOALS

SPECIAL NOTES FOR THE WEEK

NEXT LESSON

Date:

Time:

PLEASE BRING TO YOUR NEXT LESSON

PRACTICE PRIORITIES	METRONOME MARKING	TIME SPENT	TOTAL PRACTICE TIME
			day 1
PRACTICE PRIORITIES	METRONOME MARKING	TIME SPENT	TOTAL PRACTICE TIME
			day 2
PRACTICE PRIORITIES	METRONOME MARKING	TIME SPENT	TOTAL PRACTICE TIME
			day 3
PRACTICE PRIORITIES	METRONOME MARKING	TIME SPENT	TOTAL PRACTICE TIME
			day 4
PRACTICE PRIORITIES	METRONOME MARKING	TIME SPENT	TOTAL PRACTICE TIME
			day 5
PRACTICE PRIORITIES	METRONOME MARKING	TIME SPENT	TOTAL PRACTICE TIME
			day 6
PRACTICE PRIORITIES	METRONOME MARKING	TIME SPENT	TOTAL PRACTICE TIME
			day 7

WEEKLY LESSON PLAN

TODAY'S DATE: _____

SCALES AND WARMUPS	SPECIFIC GOALS

ETUDES AND EXERCISES	SPECIFIC GOALS

REPERTOIRE	SPECIFIC GOALS

OTHER	SPECIFIC GOALS

SPECIAL NOTES FOR THE WEEK

NEXT LESSON

Date:

Time:

PLEASE BRING TO YOUR NEXT LESSON

PRACTICE PRIORITIES	METRONOME MARKING	TIME SPENT	TOTAL PRACTICE TIME
			day 1
PRACTICE PRIORITIES	METRONOME MARKING	TIME SPENT	TOTAL PRACTICE TIME
			day 2
PRACTICE PRIORITIES	METRONOME MARKING	TIME SPENT	TOTAL PRACTICE TIME
			day 3
PRACTICE PRIORITIES	METRONOME MARKING	TIME SPENT	TOTAL PRACTICE TIME
			day 4
PRACTICE PRIORITIES	METRONOME MARKING	TIME SPENT	TOTAL PRACTICE TIME
			day 5
PRACTICE PRIORITIES	METRONOME MARKING	TIME SPENT	TOTAL PRACTICE TIME
			day 6
PRACTICE PRIORITIES	METRONOME MARKING	TIME SPENT	TOTAL PRACTICE TIME
			day 7